Михаил Глинка   Mikhail Glinka

(1804–1857)

ПОЛНОЕ СОБРАНИЕ СОЧИНЕНИЙ

Complete Works · Sämtliche Werke
Œuvres complètes

для фортепиано

for piano · für Klavier · pour piano

I

Urtext

Редакция · Edited by · Herausgegeben von · Edité par
Alexander Bouzovkin
K 194
Könemann Music Budapest

INDEX

Вариации

на собственную тему
Variations upon an Original Theme – Variationen über ein eigenes Thema
Variations sur un thème original

Dédiées à ... ich werde es nicht sagen

1824

Introduction

Largo

Thème

Andante espressivo

VAR. I

legato

VAR. II

con fuoco

VAR. III

Adagio

Cantabile. Molto espressivo

VAR. IV

Brillante. Vivace

A mademoiselle Lise d'Ouschakoff

Вариации

на романс "Benedetta sia la madre"
Variations upon the Song "Benedetta sia la madre"
Variationen über das Lied "Benedetta sia la madre"
Variations sur l'air "Benedetta sia la madre"

1825

Thème

VAR. I

VAR. II

Vivace

VAR. IV

Con fuoco

VAR. V
Adagio cantabile

attacca subito

VAR. VI

Tempo di polacca. En fantasie

Вариации

на русскую песню "Среди долины ровныя"
Variations upon the Russian Song "Sredi doliny rovnyya"
Variationen über das russische Lied "Sredi doliny rovnyya"
Variations sur l'air russe "Sredi doliny rovnyya"

VAR. II

Legato

dolce

28

VAR. III

Con fuoco. Più vivace

VAR. IV

Adagio. Cantabile

VAR. V

Vivace

leggiero

Вариации
на тему Моцарта
(pour piano ou harpe)
Variations upon a Mozart Theme – Variationen über ein Thema von Mozart
Variations sur un thème de Mozart

Thème

1827

VAR. II

K 194

VAR. III (pour La Harpe)

son harm.

VAR. IV (pour La Harpe)

Adagio cantabile

VAR. V

Вариации

на тему из оперы "Фаниска" Л. Керубини

Variations upon a Cherubini Theme – Variationen über ein Thema von Cherubini
Variations sur un thème de Cherubini

Thème

Moderato

1827

VAR. II

VAR. IV

Adagio cantabile

Finale

brillante

Котильон · Cotillon

1828

K 194

Мазурка   Mazurka

1828

Nocturne
(pour piano ou harpe)

1828

Moderato

Nouvelles contredanses

L'Eté

La Poule

La Trénis

Finale

Pomposo

Е.П. Штеричу

Блестящие вариации

на тему из оперы "Анна Болейн" Г. Доницетти
Brilliant Variations upon a Donizetti Theme
Brillante Variationen über ein Thema von Donizetti
Variations brillante sur un thème de Donizetti

1831

VAR. I Con moto

VAR. II

Brillante

VAR. III

Un poco meno vivo

VAR. IV

Con brio

Вариации

на две темы из балета "Chao-Kang"
Variations upon Two Dance Tunes From the Ballet "Chao-Kang"
Variationen über zwei Themen aus dem Ballett "Chao-Kang"
Variations sur deux thèmes du ballet "Chao-Kang"

1831

VAR. I

VAR. II

Thème II

VAR. I

VAR. II

Прощальный вальс

A Farawell Waltz – Abschiedswalzer – Valse d'adieu

15 июня 1831 г. Турин

K 194

Терезе Висконти д' Аррагона

Блестящее рондино
с темой В. Беллини
Brilliant Rondino with Bellini Themes
Brillantes Rondino mit Themen von Bellini
Brillant rondino avec thèmes de Bellini

1831

84

Notes

The present edition contains the complete works for the piano by M. I. Glinka in 2 volumes. The 1st volume contains his early piano compositions. The works are arranged in chronological order. The present edition is based on the autograph manuscript and/or first edition(s) of the works. Other early editions have also been consulted, whenever justified. Evident slips of pen and printing errors have been tacitly corrected. Editorial additions, reduced to a minimum, appear in square brackets. The composer's peculiarities of notation and original fingering are maintained throughout.

Variations upon an Original Theme
Autograph: SPL, estate of Glinka, catalogue No. 46.
First edition: P. Jurgenson (1878).
In autograph, Variations entitled: "Variations sur un thème composée par M. Glinka. Dédiees à ... ich werde es nicht sagen".

Variations upon the Song "Benedetta sia la madre"
Autograph: SITMC, estate of Glinka.
First edition: MUZGIZ, 1952, Complete Works for the Piano by Glinka.
In autograph, Variations entitled: "Benedetta sia la madre varié pour le pianoforte et dédie à mademoiselle Lise d'Ouschakoff par Michel Glinka amateur". The autograph dedication was crossed out by an unknown hand and did not appear in the first and following editions.

Variations upon the Russian Song "Sredi doliny rovnyya"
Autograph: SPL, estate of Glinka, catalogue No.10.
First edition: "Odeon" (P. Gurskalin, 1839).
In autograph, Variations entitled: "Air russe: Среди долины ровныя varié pour le pianoforte, composé l'an 1826".

Variations upon a Mozart Theme
Autograph: SPL, estate of Glinka, No. 190, catalogue No. 8, 10.
First edition: P. Jurgenson (1878).
The basis of the theme of the Variations is the Glockenspiel part from the finale of the first act of Mozart's opera "Die Zauberflöte". In the present edition the composition is published traditionally in the second version edited by P. Jurgenson (1878), with the addition of two variations (III, IV) from the first version edited by F. Stellovsky. The original title: "Théme de Mozart varié pour Piano-forte ou Harpe par M. Glinka (composé l'an 1822) S.P.-bourg". The exact date of the composition of the Variations (1822-1827) is not known.

Variations upon a Cherubini Theme
The autograph is lost, the composition is published from the copy made by an unknown hand with remarks by Glinka – SPL, estate of Glinka, No. 190, catalogue No. 45.
First edition: "Odeon" (P. Gurskalin, 1839).
The title of the Variations is: "Thème de l'opera "Faniska" de Cherubini (Прекрасный день) varié". In the copy of the Variations there is no title. The basis of the theme of the Variations is the introduction to the first act of the opera "Faniska" by Cherubini.

Cotillon
The autograph is lost. First edition (by M. Glinka and N. Pavlishchev): "The lyrical album of 1829". This composition is published from the first edition, SPL, estate of Glinka, catalogue No. 75.

Mazurka
The autograph is lost. First edition (by M. Glinka and N. Pavlishchev): "The lyrical album of 1829". This composition is published from the first edition, RSL.

Nocturne

Autograph: SPL, estate of Glinka, catalogue No. 10.

First edition: P. Jurgenson (1878)

New Contredanses

The autograph is lost. First edition (by M. Glinka and N. Pavlishchev): "The lyrical album of 1829". This composition is published from the first edition, RSL.

This composition in the first edition was entitled "Nouvelles contredanses". The title of the second edition is: "Французская кадриль"(on the cover-"Première contredanse").

Brilliant Variations upon a Donizetti Theme

The autograph is lost. First edition: G. Ricordi (Milan, 1831).

This composition is published from the first edition.

These Variations in the first edition were entitled: "Variazioni brillanti per pianoforte composte dal Sig. M. Glinka sul motivo dell'Aria "Nel veder tua costanza", cantata dal Celebre Sig. G. B. Rubini nell'Anna Bolena dell M° Donizetti dall'Autore dedicate al suo Amico Eugenio Steritsch Gentiluomo di Camera di Sua Maesta l'Imperatore di tutte le Russie".

Variations upon Two Dance Tunes from the Ballet "Chao-Kang"

Autograph: Library of Stanford University (USA).

First edition: G. Ricordi (Milan, 1831). This composition is published from the first edition.

In the first edition the Variations were entitled: "Due ballabili nel baletto Chao-Kang variati per pianoforte e dedicati a sua eccellenza il Sig-re conte Woronzow-Daschkow dal Sig-re M. Glinka".

A Farewell Waltz

The autograph is lost. First edition in the magazine "Eol's harp", No. 6 (1833-34), SPL (St. Petersburg).

This composition is published from the first edition.

Brilliant Rondino on a Bellini Theme

The autograph is lost. First edition: G. Ricordi (Milan, 1832). This composition is published from the first edition.

The first edition is entitled: "Rondino brillante per pianoforte nel quale è introdotto il motivo 'La tremenda ultrice spada' del M° Bellini. Composto e dedicato a donna Teresa Visconti d'Arragona da M. Glinka".

ABBREVIATIONS

1. **SPL** State Public Library (St. Petersburg)
2. **RSL** Russian State Library (Moscow)
3. **SITMC** State Institute of Theater, Music and Cinema (St. Petersburg)

Mikhail Ivanovich Glinka was born on June 9, 1804 in Novospasskoye, on the estate of his parents, a rich family of landowners. He was educated at home till 1818. The home education of Russian rich families was extensive. Glinka studied French, mathematics, drawing and music with a young teacher Varvara Klammer. His music studies were successful: soon he could play four hands with his sister some overtures, symphonies and fragments from operas. The musical impressions of the young Glinka were various. He heard a lot of Russian folk songs in the countryside, where he lived; he also heard the best compositions of European music. The family liked music and often during parties there was not only piano or vocal music, but the private orchestra of their nearest relatives the Shmakovs also often played. One of his greatest musical impressions in childhood was the performance by musicians of this orchestra of a quartet by Bernhardt Krusel. From 1818 Glinka continued his education at an exclusive school in St. Petersburg. He also took private lessons in music. His piano teacher was a resident German musician, Carl Meyer. When the famous pianist John Field was in St. Petersburg, Glinka had an opportunity to study with him. Glinka began to compose even before acquiring adequate training in theory.

After leaving the Noble Pansion (the exclusive school at St. Petersburg University) he was faced with a choice of career. It was considered below the dignity of a gentleman to become a professional musician, and Glinka entered the Ministry of Communications in St. Petersburg in 1824. Certainly he was not satisfied in his job. He constantly improved his general education by reading, studied music, and took singing lessons with an Italian teacher, Belloni. Glinka's soft voice (tenor) was very expressive. His friends – the best Russian writers and musicians, Zhukovsky, Pushkin, Viyelgorsky and Odoyevsky appreciated his playing and singing. Glinka remained in the government service until 1828. He felt that his musical education was not sufficient for his creative ambitions. In 1830 he went to Italy, where he continued intermittent studies in Milan. Glinka travelled in Italy, collecting folk songs, visiting Naples, Rome and Bologna. It was during these trips that he met Mendelssohn, Berlioz, Donizetti and Bellini, and became enchanted by Italian music. His early vocal and instrumental compositions are thoroughly Italian in melodic and harmonic structure (especially the piano compositions).

In 1833 Glinka went to Berlin to take a course in counterpoint and general composition with the famous German theorist Siegfried Dehn. He was nearly 30 when he completed his theoretical education. In 1834 his father died and Glinka went back to Russia to take care of the family affairs. In the winter of 1834-35 Glinka often visited Vassily Zhukovsky, the famous Russian poet. At his parties Glinka met the cream of St. Petersburg society: writers, artists, musicians. They talked of Russia, its history and culture, and the idea of creating really Russian national professional music was born in Glinka's mind. The return to his native land led him to consider the composition of a truly national opera on a subject (suggested to him by Zhukovsky) depicting an episode from Russian history, the saving of the first Tsar of the Romanoff dynasty by a common peasant, Ivan Susanin. Glinka's first opera was produced in St. Petersburg on December 9, 1836, under the title "A life for the Tsar". The event was hailed by the literary and artistic circles of Russia as a milestone in Russian culture, and indeed the entire development of Russian national music received its decisive creative impulse from Glinka's patriotic opera.

In 1835 Glinka married Maria Petrovna Ivanovna, but the marriage was unhappy, and they soon separated, a final divorce coming in 1846.

His next opera "Rouslan and Ludmila", based on Pushkin's fairy tale, was produced on December 9, 1842. This opera too became extremely popular in Russia. Glinka introduced into the score many elements of Oriental music. Both operas retain the traditional Italian form, with arias, choruses and orchestral episodes clearly separated.

In 1842 Liszt visited Russia and heard Glinka's music. He was tremendously impressed and wrote a transcription of the "March of Chernomor" for piano. Glinka also travelled in Spain, where he collected folk songs. The result of Glinka's researches in new orchestral style was two overtures "Jota Aragonesa" and "The summer night in Madrid". On his way back to Russia he stayed in Warsaw for three years. The remaining years of his life he spent in St. Petersburg, Paris and Berlin. In St. Petersburg Glinka composed a lot of romances and began a new symphony "Taras Bulba" on the subject of Gogol's novel. He helped two young Russian composers, Dargomyzhsky and Balakirev. On February 15, 1857 Glinka died in Berlin.

After Glinka's death, Dargomyzhsky and Balakirev continued the development of Russian national music.

Pushkin is called "the sun of Russian poetry" and Glinka – "the Pushkin of music".

© 1997 for this edition by Könemann Music Budapest Kft.
H-1093 Budapest, Közraktár utca 10.

K 194

Distributed worldwide by
Könemann Verlagsgesellschaft mbH, Bonner Str. 126.
D-50968 Köln

Responsible co-editor: Vladimir Ryabov
Production: Detlev Schaper
Cover design: Peter Feierabend
Technical editor: Dezső Varga

Engraved in Moscow, Russia

Printed by Kossuth Printing House Co., Budapest
Printed in Hungary

ISBN 963 8303 88 3